TABLE OF CONTENT

TABLE OF CONTENT 2

1. STRAWBERRY ICE CREAM 4
2. ORANGE MARMALADE 4
3. GLUTEN-FREE HOLIDAY BLISS COOKIE BARS 6
4. BLACKBERRY DUMP CAKE 7
5. AIR FRYER CHERRY CREAM CHEESE CROISSANTS 8
6. HOMEMADE STRAWBERRY CRUMBLE 9
7. CANTALOUPE FRENZY 10
8. BLUEBERRY CREAM CHEESE WONTONS 10
9. BALSAMIC BRAISED PORK TENDERLOINS WITH FRESH FIGS 12
10. AIR FRYER GRILLED PEVERYES WITH CINNAMON 13
11. APRICOT AND PEVERY FRIED PIES 14
12. BACON-WRAPPED CHERRIES 15
13. POMEGRANATE SHERBET 15
14. SPICED PEAR OLD-FASHIONED 16
15. GRILLED HALLOUMI WITH HERBED BERRY SALSA 17
16. PB & J SMOOTHIE 18
17. INSTANT POT PEVERY COBBLER 19
18. APPLE-CRANBERRY CROSTADA 20
19. SWEET POTATO CRUNCH 21
20. CRANBERRY PUMPKIN COOKIES 22
21. BEST STRAWBERRY DAIQUIRI 23
22. EASY APPLE CIDER 24
23. SEVEN LAYER BARS 24
24. CRUSTLESS CRANBERRY PIE 25
25. BROWN SUGAR AND PINEAPPLE GLAZED HAM 26
26. EASY CRANBERRY ORANGE RELISH 27
27. HAM WITH PINEAPPLE 27
28. SPINACH AND BANANA POWER SMOOTHIE 28
29. GINGERBREAD COOKIE FROSTING 29
30. CARAMEL APPLES 30

31. PINEAPPLE STUFFING 30
32. AWESOME SAUSAGE, APPLE AND CRANBERRY STUFFING 31
33. AMAZING APPLE BUTTER 32
34. CRANBERRY ORANGE BREAD 33
35. GREEK LEMON CHICKEN SOUP 34
36. HOMEMADE BANANA PUDDING 36
37. FRESH CRANBERRY SAUCE 36
38. BANANA PUMPKIN BREAD 37
39. SPINACH AND STRAWBERRY SALAD 38
40. DELICIOUS CINNAMON BAKED APPLES 39
41. CHICKEN WITH LEMON-CAPER SAUCE 40
42. BLUEBERRY SIMPLE SYRUP 41
43. HOT SPIKED CIDER 42
44. ALMOST NO FAT BANANA BREAD 43
45. THREE BERRY PIE 44
46. LEMON-ORANGE ORANGE ROUGHY 45
47. IRISH POTATO CANDY 46
48. DUTCH APPLE PIE WITH OATMEAL STREUSEL 46
49. MINCEMEAT 48
50. BEST BOILED FRUITCAKE 49

1. STRAWBERRY ICE CREAM

Prep Time:25 mins

Cook Time:15 mins

Additional Time:1 hrs

Total Time:1 hrs 40 mins

Ingredients

- 1 quart fresh strawberries, hulled
- 1 ½ cups of heavy cream, separated
- ¾ cup of white sugar
- 3 egg yolks
- 3 tbsp light corn syrup

Directions

1. Strawberries should be added to a blender or food processor container and pureed until smooth. Pour into a large basin and reserve.

2. 1 1/4 cups of cream should be heated in a saucepan over medium heat until it bubbles around the pan's edge. In a big bowl, mix the sugar, egg yolks, remaining 1/4 cup of cream, and corn syrup. While continuously whisking, slowly pour the heated cream into the egg yolk mixture. Return the mixture to the pan and cook for about 5 minutes, or until it is thick enough to coat the back of a metal spoon. Don't let the mixture come to a boil. In a sieve, mix custard and berry purée. Refrigerate until cooled.

3. The liquid should be poured into an ice cream machine and refrigerated in accordance with the manufacturer's instructions.

2. ORANGE MARMALADE

Cook Time:1 hrs 25 mins

Soak Time:8 hrs

Total Time:9 hrs 55 mins

Servings:32

Ingredients

- 5 small navel oranges (about 2 1/4 lb. total), washed and scrubbed
- 1 medium (5 oz.) lemon, washed and scrubbed
- 6 cups of water
- 3 ½ cups of granulated sugar

Directions

1. Orange and lemon tops and bottoms should be slice off and discarded. 3 of the oranges' skins and pith should be peel off off and discarded. All oranges and lemons should be slice into quarters lengthwise, then every quarter should be lightly split into 1/8-inch slices. All of the citrus slices should be put in a big basin with water. For at least 8 hours and up to 24 hours, cover and chill.

2. In a big stainless steel Dutch oven or saucepan, add water, orange, and lemon slices. Using a high heat, bring to a boil. After it reaches a rolling boil, lower the heat to medium and simmer, covered, stirring regularly, for 45 minutes, or until the orange rinds have softened and can be split with a spoon with only a little resistance. During this time, skim off any foam that accumulates on the surface.

3. Examine the rings of 4 (1/2-pint) canning jars for rust and cracks; discard any that are damaged. Place in simmering water until ready to make orange marmalade. With warm, soapy water, clean new, unused lids and rings. A small plate should be put in the freezer.

4. Mixture of oranges and sugar is then brought to a boil over high heat. Cook, sometimes stirring, for 40 to 45 minutes, or until a thermometer registers 220 degrees F (104 degrees C), the liquid has somewhat reduced, and the bubbles in the center are slightly larger. During this time, the mixture will spend the majority of its time between 212 degrees Fahrenheit (100 degrees C) and 216 degrees Fahrenheit (102 degrees C), only rising to 220 degrees Fahrenheit (104 degrees C) when enough liquid has evaporated.

5. Take the dish out of the freezer and spoon a small quantity of marmalade onto it to see if the consistency is right. Re-freeze the plate for one minute. Take the dish out of the freezer and drag your finger across the plate and through the jam. It ought to leave a spotless trace. If the jam is runny and does not leave a clear trail, bring the mixture back to a boil over medium-high, then place the dish back in the freezer. Cook marmalade for three minutes while stirring frequently. Remove from heat, and if required, continue the process until the desired thickness is reached.

6. Spread out the marmalade carefully into the ready canning jars. Uncovered, allow it cool to ambient temperature for about three hours. Jars should be sealed. at least two hours, or until marmalade sets, chill. Keep chilled for up to two weeks.

7. Cook's Notes: The marmalade needs to be carefully canned if you intend to keep it for a long period. Empty jars without lids or bands should be placed into simmering water using tongs. Jars should be placed in a pot on their sides so that water can fill them. Turn jars upside down with a jar lifter. Boil for 10 minutes at a moderate boil over high heat, adjusting heat as necessary to maintain the gentle boil. Jars should be removed from the pot using a jar lifter, allowing water to return to the pot. Jars should be put on a fresh kitchen towel. Take the pot off the stove and cover it to keep the water warm for the final canning stage.

8. In a sizable, deep skillet, arrange the jar bands and lids. Add water until it is covered by 1/2 inch. On medium-high, simmer the water. Get rid of the heat. (Overheating will deteriorate rubber and the effectiveness of the lids' seal.)

9. Making use of a canning funnel to keep the jar rims spotless and leaving a 1/4-inch headspace, ladle hot marmalade into hot, sterilized jars. Wipe the jar rims with a damp paper towel while wearing gloves. Lift lids out of boiling water using a magnetic lid lifter and place them on jars. Bands for jars should be tight enough to pinch. (Be careful not to overtighten; the jars need room for the air to escape. Jar seals will break or jars can split if jar bands are overly tight.)

10. Making ensuring the jars are standing properly on the canning rack and not contacting one another or the pot's sides, lower them into the hot water using the jar lifter. Make sure jars have 1 to 2 inches of water in them (add hot water if needed).

11. On high heat, bring to a vigorous boil. Boil for 10 minutes while covered. After taking it off the heat, let it stand for 10 minutes. Remove the jars from the pot using a jar lifter, and set them 1 inch apart on a clean kitchen towel. Let 3 hours to reach room temperature.

12. Lids on safe preservation jars should curve inward when they warm up to room temperature. Jars should be cleaned and given a name and date label. Keep any improperly sealed jars in the refrigerator for up to two weeks. For up to a year, sealed jars can be kept in a cold, dark location.

3. GLUTEN-FREE HOLIDAY BLISS COOKIE BARS

Prep Time:20 mins

Cook Time:25 mins

Additional Time:30 mins

Total Time:1 hrs 15 mins

Ingredients

- 1 cup of unsalted butter, softened
- ¾ cup of brown sugar
- ½ cup of white sugar
- 2 large eggs
- 1 tsp ground cinnamon
- 1 tsp vanilla extract
- 2 ½ cups of gluten-free flour blend (such as Namaste Perfect Flour Blend™)
- 1 tsp baking soda

- 1 tsp salt
- ½ tsp xanthan gum
- 1 (8 ounce) package white chocolate chips
- ¾ cup of shredded coconut
- 1 (16 ounce) container cream cheese frosting
- ½ cup of chop up dried cranberries, or as need

Directions

1. Set the oven to 350 degrees Fahrenheit (175 degrees C). A 9x13-inch pan should be buttered.
2. In a bowl, mix the butter, brown sugar, white sugar, eggs, cinnamon, and vanilla essence. Mix well.
3. In a separate basin, mix the flour, baking soda, salt, and xanthan gum. Mix thoroughly after adding half of the flour mixture to the egg mixture. Add the remaining flour mixture, white chocolate chips, and coconut to the mixture. Mix thoroughly. Into the prepared pan, press.
4. At 23 minutes into baking, the edges should begin to brown in the preheated oven. Let 30 minutes for the cooling to complete.
5. Cranberry chunks are added after frosting with cream cheese. Make 48 triangles by sliceting.

Cook's Note:

- These cookies can be baked in individual portions. 12 minutes or so in the oven, or until the edges are golden.

4. BLACKBERRY DUMP CAKE

Prep Time:10 mins

Cook Time:45 mins

Total Time:55 mins

Servings:12

Ingredients

- 4 ½ cups of fresh blackberries
- 1 ½ cups of white sugar
- 1 cup of unsalted butter, thinly split
- 1 (15.25 ounce) package French vanilla cake mix

Directions

1. Set the oven to 350 degrees Fahrenheit (175 degrees C).
2. Blackberries and sugar should be mixd in a bowl. Spread evenly over the bottom of a 9x13-inch glass baking pan after transferring.
3. Over the berries, evenly distribute the cake mix. Butter slices should cover the majority of the cake mix as you distribute them equally over it. Never mix or stir.
4. Bake for about 45 minutes, or until topping is golden brown, in a preheated oven. Serve hot.

Note from the Chef:

- You can use 4 to 5 cups of fresh blackberries.

5. AIR FRYER CHERRY CREAM CHEESE CROISSANTS

Prep Time:10 mins

Cook Time:5 mins

Total Time:15 mins

Ingredients

- 1 (8 ounce) package refrigeratedd crescent roll dough (such as Pillsbury®
- 1 (8 ounce) tub cream cheese
- 1 (15 ounce) can pitted sour cherries, drained
- cooking spray
- ground cinnamon as need

Directions

1. Dust a work surface with flour very lightly. Triangles made of unrolled crescent dough should be slice along the perforated lines.
2. Cream cheese should be spread on every triangle.

3. Every triangle of crescent-shaped dough should have 3 or 4 cherries placed on the wider side. Every crescent should be carefully rolled up, with the cherries nestled in. Every roll's ends should be slightly lowered to create a crescent shape.

4. Put non-stick cooking spray to the air fryer's basket. Place the croissants into the basket with care.

5. Preheat air fryer to 400 degrees Fahrenheit (200 degrees C).

6. For about 5 minutes, air fry croissants until they are puffy and lightly browned. Make sure the croissants aren't clinging to one another and aren't getting too browned. Make sure they don't get too done by cooking for an additional 2 to 3 minutes.

7. Spread cinnamon over the croissants after transferring them to a platter.

Cook's Note:

- Cherry pie filling can be used for canned cherries.

6. HOMEMADE STRAWBERRY CRUMBLE

Prep Time: 15 mins

Cook Time: 45 mins

Additional Time: 10 mins

Total Time: 1 hrs 10 mins

Servings: 8

Ingredients

- 1 cup of all-purpose flour
- ¾ cup of old-fashioned rolled oats
- ¾ cup of chop up walnuts
- 1 ½ tsp ground ginger
- 1 cup of packed light brown sugar, separated
- ½ cup of salted butter, melted
- 2 tbsp cornstarch
- 2 tbsp white balsamic vinegar
- 2 ½ pounds fresh strawberries, hulled and quartered

- vanilla ice cream, for serving

Directions

1. Set the oven to 350 degrees Fahrenheit (175 degrees C). An 11x7-inch baking dish should be greased.

2. In a bowl, mix flour, ginger, oats, walnuts, and 3/4 cup of brown sugar. Add the butter and mix with your hands until the mixture is wet and resembles coarse crumbs.

3. In a sizable bowl, mix the cornstarch, vinegar, and remaining 1/4 cup of brown sugar. Toss in the strawberries. Add to the baking dish that has been prepared and cover with crumble mixture.

4. Bake for 45 to 50 minutes, or until the strawberries are soft, the mixture is rapidly bubbling around the edges, and the top is brown.

5. Remove from oven and wait for about 10 minutes till room temperature. With vanilla ice cream, serve warm.

7. CANTALOUPE FRENZY

Prep Time:7 mins

Cook Time:2 mins

Total Time:9 mins

Servings:3

Ingredients

- 1 cantaloupe - peel off, seeded and cubed
- 3 tbsp white sugar, or as need
- 2 cups of ice cubes

Directions

1. Cantaloupe cubes and ice should be added to the blender's container. Once the ice is broken up, process. Puree after adding sugar. Pour the mixture into tall glasses and serve right away.

8. BLUEBERRY CREAM CHEESE WONTONS

Prep Time:30 mins

Cook Time:5 mins

Total Time: 35 mins

Servings: 48

Ingredients

- ½ (8 ounce) package cream cheese
- 48 wonton wrappers
- 1 cup of blueberry pie filling
- water as needed
- cooking spray
- ¼ cup of powdered sugar

Directions

2. To make 4 pieces, slice a 4 ounce block of cream cheese in half twice. To create 8 equal pieces overall, slice every component once more in half. Set aside.
3. Separate out six wonton wrappers at a time onto a spotless work area. Every wonton wrapper should have a slice of cream cheese in the center. Split one of the cream cheese pieces into six equal pieces. Top the cream cheese with 1 tsp of blueberry pie filling. A full container may cause the substance to flow out.
4. Every wonton wrapper's four edges should be lightly moistened with your finger. To create a triangle, gently fold in half diagonally. Next, raise the remaining two corners so that they meet. Avoid leaving the wontons with too much air because this could make them rupture. To ensure a tight seal, press the seams together. While you finish creating the remaining wontons, place the wontons in a container and cover with a damp paper towel.
5. Set the air fryer to 325 degrees Fahrenheit (160 degrees C). As many wontons as will fit in the inside basket without overcrowding should be placed there after spraying it with cooking spray. Spray cooking spray on the wontons sparingly.
6. For five minutes, air fry. Transfer to a cooling rack and sprinkle with confectioners' sugar. When cooking the remaining wontons in batches, allow to cool. Best served at room temperature or slightly heated.

Kitchen Notes:

- I've successfully put these together up to 8 hours in advance. Put in a sealed container in the refrigerator in a single layer with a damp paper towel covering it until you're ready to air fry. Moreover, you can freeze them raw. Add one minute to the cook time if you're preparing them from refrigerated.

- You can also prepare them in the oven if you don't have an air fryer. Wontons should be arranged in a single layer on a baking sheet, coated with cooking spray, and baked for 8 to 10 minutes at 375°F (190°C).
- It takes 48 tsp of pie filling to make one cup of. To allow for error, you might wish to start with a little more pie filling.

9. BALSAMIC BRAISED PORK TENDERLOINS WITH FRESH FIGS

Prep Time:15 mins

Cook Time:45 mins

Total Time:1 hrs

Ingredients

- 2 (1 1/2 pound) pork tenderloins
- 1 tsp kosher salt, or as need
- ½ tsp freshly ground black pepper, or as need
- 2 tbsp olive oil
- 2 shallots, thinly split lengthwise
- 12 fresh figs, stemmed and halved
- 1 cup of chicken broth
- ¼ cup of good-quality balsamic vinegar
- 1 tbsp chop up fresh rosemary
- fresh rosemary sprigs for garnish (non-compulsory)

Directions

1. Set the oven to 350 degrees Fahrenheit (175 degrees C).
2. Remove any silver skin from the tenderloins after patting them dry. As need, add freshly ground pepper and kosher salt.
3. Oil should shimmer after being heated over medium heat in a sizable oven-safe skillet. Tenderloins should be carefully placed into the heated oil and browned for 7 to 10 minutes total, on both sides.

4. Around the tenderloins, add the slice shallots and stir for approximately a minute. Figs, chicken broth, and balsamic vinegar should all be added. The moment the mixture starts to bubble, cover everything with chop up rosemary.

5. For 25 to 30 minutes, or until the pork is no longer pink in the center, bake the dish covered in the preheated oven. The inside temperature should register 145 degrees Fahrenheit on an instant-read thermometer (63 degrees C).

6. Pork should be taken out of the skillet with tongs and placed on a serving dish. Place the figs all over the tenderloins after removing them from the skillet with a slotted spoon. Wrap it up loosely with foil.

7. Return the skillet to the stovetop and heat it to a medium-high setting. During the next 10 to 15 minutes, boil the pan juices until they have reduced to approximately 3/4 cup of.

8. Split tenderloins should be topped with reduced liquid, drizzled with fresh rosemary sprigs, if preferred.

9. Use pork loins that weigh between one and five pounds.

10. AIR FRYER GRILLED PEVERYES WITH CINNAMON

Prep Time:5 mins

Cook Time:12 mins

Cool Time:5 mins

Total Time:22 mins

Ingredients

- 1 medium firm peach, halved and pitted
- 2 tbsp unsalted butter
- 1 tsp light brown sugar
- ¼ tsp ground cinnamon
- 2 scoops vanilla ice cream

Directions

1. Set air fryer to 350 degrees Fahrenheit (175 degrees C).

2. Put peach halves, flesh side down, in the air fryer's basket. For six minutes, cook.

3. Melt butter while waiting. Brown sugar and cinnamon are added; stir until sugar is melted.

4. Flip peaches over so that the flesh side is facing up using tongs. Apply the butter mixture to the top, letting any extra drip into the pit hollow. Cook for a further 6 minutes.

5. Let peaches five minutes to cool. Add an ice cream scoop to the top of every half. Serve right away.

11. APRICOT AND PEVERY FRIED PIES

Cook Time:30 mins

Total Time:30 mins

Servings:18

Ingredients

Dough:

- 4 cups of all-purpose flour
- 2 tsp salt
- 1 cup of shortening
- 1 cup of milk

Filling:

- 8 ounces dried apricots
- 1 (6 ounce) package dried peaches
- ¾ cup of white sugar
- water to cover
- 2 cups of vegetable oil for frying

Directions

1. Flour and salt should be mixd in a sizable bowl to make the crust. Add shortening and mix until crumbly. Add milk and continue stirring until dough forms a ball. Slice out 18 6-inch circles from rolled-out dough. Set aside.

2. Making Filling Mix sugar, peaches, and apricots in a big pot. The fruit should be covered with water. Cook covered pan over low heat until fruit begins to crumble. Take off the top and keep cooking until all the water has evaporated.

3. Little high-sided skillet with oil or shortening should be used. Put in a medium-hot area. Fill every pastry circle with an equal quantity of filling, then fold in half. With a fork dipped in cold water, seal the pastry.

4. Many pies should be fried at once in hot oil, browning both sides. On paper towels, drip-dry pies.

Cook's Tip:

- Melt shortening, such as Crisco®, so that it is two inches deep.

- Editor's note: Based on a 10% retention value following cooking, we calculated the nutritional value of oil for frying. The precise amount may change based on the density of the ingredients, cook time and temperature, and the particular oil used.

12. BACON-WRAPPED CHERRIES

Prep Time:20 mins

Cook Time:5 mins

Total Time:25 mins

Ingredients

- 36 maraschino cherries, stemmed, drained and juice reserved
- 18 slices bacon slices, halved
- 36 toothpicks

Directions

1. Preheat the oven's broiler while positioning the oven rack about 6 inches from the heat source.
2. Every cherry should be wrapped in a half of bacon, fastened with a toothpick, and placed on a baking pan. Overwrapped cherries, drizzle reserved cherry juice.
3. For three to ten minutes, broil the bacon in a preheated oven until it is crisp to your preference.

Tips

- If you prefer your bacon crisp, the cooking time can be extended, but I believe that soft bacon is preferable.

- This dish would also work well on a grill with a grate that is tiny enough so that the cherries don't fall through, however I haven't tested it.

13. POMEGRANATE SHERBET

Prep Time: 10 mins

Cook Time: 2 mins

Freeze Time: 3 hrs 30 mins

Total Time: 3 hrs 42 mins

Ingredients

- 3 cups of unsweetened pomegranate juice
- 1 cup of sugar
- 3 tbsp lemon juice
- 1 dash salt
- ¼ cup of cold water
- 1 (.25 ounce) envelope unflavored gelatin
- 1 cup of chilled whipping cream

Directions

1. In a sizable bowl, mix the salt, sugar, lemon juice, and pomegranate juice. 30 minutes of covered chilling.

2. Gelatin should be added to the cold water in a small saucepan. Let stand for one minute. Just whisk over low heat for 2 minutes to help the gelatin dissolve. Add to pomegranate mixture by stirring. Add the cream, and whip the mixture for about 3 minutes at medium speed with an electric hand mixer.

3. Sherbet should be refrigerated in an ice cream maker for one to one and a half hours, or until it has a soft-serve consistency.

4. Add to a container that can be refrigerated that is 1 or 2 qt. Directly cover the surface with a piece of plastic wrap, then freeze for at least two hours or for up to one month.

14. SPICED PEAR OLD-FASHIONED

Prep Time: 5 mins

Total Time: 5 mins

Ingredients

- ¼ pear, chop up

- 2 sprigs fresh rosemary, separated
- 1 lemon twist
- 1 tsp pure maple syrup
- 3 dashes cardamom bitters
- 1 ½ fluid ounces bourbon
- ½ fluid ounce ginger liqueur (such as Domaine de Canton®)
- 1 cup of ice cubes
- 3 ounces club soda, chilled
- 1 very large ice cube
- 1 pear wedge for garnish

Directions

1. Using a muddler or the handle of a wooden spoon, muddle the chop up pear, 1 rosemary sprig, lemon twist, maple syrup, and bitters in a cocktail shaker until the pear is liquid. To the cocktail shaker, add the bourbon, ginger liqueur, and 1 cup of ice. Shake the cover until well cooled.

2. Set a small, fine strainer over the glass after adding a huge ice cube to the rocks glass. To remove any significant pulp or rosemary pieces, strain the beverage through the sieve and cocktail shaker top. Add club soda on top. Pear wedge and rosemary sprig for garnish.

15. GRILLED HALLOUMI WITH HERBED BERRY SALSA

Prep Time: 20 mins

Cook Time: 15 mins

Total Time: 35 mins

Servings:4

Ingredients

- 4 ounces fresh blueberries
- 3 ounces red currants
- 3 tbsp chop up fresh mint, separated
- 3 tbsp chop up fresh cilantro, separated
- 1 tbsp fresh marjoram, stems removed
- 1 habanero pepper, seeded and chop up
- 2 tbsp olive oil
- 2 tbsp agave syrup
- 2 limes, separated
- ½ cup of cashews
- 8 ounces halloumi cheese, slice into 8 slices

Directions

1. In a mixing bowl, mix blueberries and red currants. Add 1 lime juice, 2 tsp every of mint, cilantro, marjoram, and habanero. Also include olive oil and agave syrup. mix, then reserve.
2. A nonstick griddle should be heated to medium-high heat. Sauté cashews for 8 to 10 minutes, turning frequently to prevent burning, until they are browned. Put cashews on a platter and reserve. Halloumi cheese slices should be browned for two to three minutes on every side at medium heat.
3. Put the halloumi cheese on a platter and garnish with the remaining 1 tbsp of mint and cilantro as well as the berry salsa combination. Spread chop up cashews over the halloumi. Add lime wedges from the remaining lime as a garnish. Serve right away.

16. PB & J SMOOTHIE

Prep Time:5 mins

Total Time:5 mins

Servings:1

Ingredients

- 6 refrigerated strawberries, or more as need
- ¾ cup of milk
- 1 ½ tbsp peanut butter
- 1 tbsp blue agave nectar, or more as need
- 1 tbsp flax seeds

Directions

1. Blend strawberries, milk, peanut butter, blue agave, and flax seeds thoroughly in a blender.

Kitchen Notes:

- If preferred, you can swap out the peanut butter for 2 tbsp of powdered peanut butter and 1 1/2 tbsp of water.
- Ice is not needed if refrigerated strawberries are used. Blackberries, raspberries, or blueberries can be used in place of the strawberries.
- You can use any type of nut or dairy milk.

17. INSTANT POT PEVERY COBBLER

Prep Time:10 mins

Cook Time:25 mins

Additional Time:25 mins

Total Time:1 hrs

Ingredients

- 3 (15 ounce) cans peaches, drained
- 1 tsp cinnamon sugar
- 1 ½ cups of white cake mix
- ¼ tsp ground cinnamon
- 4 tbsp unsalted butter
- ½ cup of water

Directions

2. Peveryes should be drained and dried using paper towels. Sprinkle cinnamon sugar on the peaches.

3. Mix cinnamon into dry cake mix. Mixture should resemble coarse crumbs after adding butter. Put aside half of the mixture.

4. Place peaches in a 6-inch circular dish after combining them with half of the cake mix mixture. Add the remaining cake batter on top of the peaches. Wrap the dish in foil.

5. Fill a multipurpose pressure cooker with water (such as Instant Pot). Trivet should be inside. Put a circular dish atop the trivet. Lock the lid by closing it. Set the timer for 12 minutes while choosing high pressure in accordance with the manufacturer's recommendations. Give the pressure 10 to 15 minutes to build.

6. In accordance with the manufacturer's recommendations, release pressure naturally over a period of 20 minutes. Lock released, lid removed. Using the quick-release technique, quickly relieve any leftover pressure; this will take around 5 minutes.

7. Preheat the oven's broiler to high and place a rack about 6 inches from the heat source.

8. Dish should be carefully taken out of the pot and exposed. Around 2 minutes of broiling will set the topping.

18. APPLE-CRANBERRY CROSTADA

Ingredients

- 3 tbsp butter
- 2 pounds Granny Smith apples (or other firm, crisp apples), peel off, quartered, cored and split 1/4-inch thick
- 1 pound Macintosh apples (or other soft-textured apples that fall apart when cooked), peel off, quartered, cored, and split 1/4-inch thick
- ½ cup of sugar
- ½ cup of dried cranberries
- 1 sheet refrigerated puff pastry, thawed but still cold (follow package directions)
- 1 egg white, lightly beaten
- 1 tbsp sugar
- 1 cup of Non-compulsory: Ice cream or lightly sweetened whipped cream

Directions

1. In a sizable skillet set over medium-high heat, melt the butter. Add the apples, 1/2 cup of sugar, and cranberries. Cover the pan and heat for 5 minutes, or until the apples start to release their liquid.

Remove the lid and continue to cook, stirring regularly, for an additional 5 minutes, or until the juices have thickened to the consistency of thin syrup and the soft apples have crumbled. Pour into a pan with a wide lip, such as a jellyroll pan, and allow to cool to room temperature. (May be kept chilled for up to five days in an airtight container.)

2. Heat the oven to 400 degrees and lower the oven rack. Puff pastry sheet spread open on a work surface dusted with fine flour. 10 by 16-inch rectangle formed by rolling. Place on a big cookie sheet. (I advise coating the baking sheet with parchment paper; this prevents the crostada from sticking and makes cleanup simple.)

3. Using a 2-inch border, spread cooked apples over the crust. Over apples, fold up the pastry borders. To prevent dough from overlapping, unfold the corners and create ruffled creases. Apply egg white to the pastry border and then top with the final tbsp of sugar. Bake for 25 to 30 minutes, or until pastry is golden brown. Serve hot or room temperature with whipped cream or ice cream as desired.

Tips

- Pam Anderson, a columnist for USA WEEKEND, 2004. Toutes droits réservés.

19. SWEET POTATO CRUNCH

Prep Time: 15 mins

Cook Time: 1 hrs 30 mins

Total Time: 1 hrs 45 mins

Servings: 10

Ingredients

- 6 sweet potatoes
- ⅓ cup of butter
- 2 tbsp white sugar
- ½ cup of milk
- 2 large eggs, beaten
- 1 tsp vanilla extract
- Crunch Topping:
- ¾ cup of brown sugar
- ¾ cup of sweetened flaked coconut

- ¾ cup of chop up pecans
- 3 tbsp all-purpose flour
- 3 tbsp melted butter

Directions

1. To boil, add salted water to a big saucepan with the sweet potatoes inside. Simmer for 20 to 30 minutes over medium-low heat until fork-tender. Peel and drain.

2. Set the oven to 325 degrees Fahrenheit (165 degrees C).

3. In a bowl, mix sweet potatoes, 1/3 cup of butter, and white sugar. Using an electric mixer, mix sweet potato mixture, milk, eggs, and vanilla; blend until smooth. Spoon half of the mixture into a 9x13-inch casserole dish.

4. Creating the topping In a bowl, mix flour, brown sugar, coconut, and pecans. Add 3 tbsp of melted butter and whisk to mix. Over the sweet potato mixture in the baking dish, distribute half of the topping. Sprinkle the remaining topping over the leftover sweet potato mixture.

5. Bake for about an hour in the preheated oven, or until thoroughly heated through and topping is gently browned.

20. CRANBERRY PUMPKIN COOKIES

Prep Time: 20 mins

Cook Time: 15 mins

Total Time: 35 mins

Servings: 36

Ingredients

- 1 cup of white sugar
- ½ cup of butter, softened
- 1 cup of solid pack pumpkin puree
- 1 large egg
- 1 tsp vanilla extract
- 2 ¼ cups of all-purpose flour
- 2 tsp baking powder

- 1 tsp baking soda
- 1 tsp ground cinnamon
- ½ tsp salt
- 1 cup of halved fresh cranberries
- ½ cup of chop up walnuts
- 1 tbsp orange zest

Directions

1. Set the oven to 375 degrees Fahrenheit (190 degrees C). Make two cookie sheets greased.
2. Using an electric mixer, cream the butter and sugar in a big bowl until frothy. Mix vanilla, egg, and pumpkin purée.
3. In a larger basin, mix the flour, salt, baking soda, cinnamon, and baking powder. Blend the flour mixture and pumpkin mixture thoroughly. Add the orange zest, walnuts, and cranberries. Put tspfuls of dough onto the prepared baking sheets, spacing them apart by 2 inches.
4. Bake for 10 to 12 minutes, or until the edges are brown in the preheated oven.
5. Transfer to wire racks to cool after being taken out of the oven.

21. BEST STRAWBERRY DAIQUIRI

Prep Time: 10 mins

Total Time: 10 mins

Servings: 8

Ingredients

- 4 ounces refrigerated strawberries
- ½ cup of white sugar
- ½ cup of lemon juice
- ⅛ cup of lime juice
- ¾ cup of rum
- ¼ cup of lemon-lime flavored carbonated beverage

- 6 cups of ice, or as needed

Directions

1. Blended refrigerated strawberries with sugar, lime juice, and lemon juice. Add ice after adding the rum and lemon-lime beverage. Once smooth, blend.

Tips

- If you have access to fresh, in-season strawberries, use them!

22. EASY APPLE CIDER

Prep Time:10 mins

Cook Time:1 hrs

Total Time:1 hrs 10 mins

Ingredients

- 1 (64 fluid ounce) bottle apple cider
- 3 cinnamon sticks
- 1 tsp whole allspice
- 1 tsp whole cloves
- ⅓ cup of brown sugar

Directions

2. In a slow cooker, mix apple cider and cinnamon sticks.
3. An 8-inch square of cheesecloth should have cloves and spices in the center. Place the cheesecloth in the slow cooker after gathering the edges and tying them together. Add brown sugar and mix. To boil, continue to cook on high. Turn the thermostat down to low and stay warm.

23. SEVEN LAYER BARS

Prep Time:15 mins

Cook Time:25 mins

Additional Time:20 mins

Total Time:1 hrs

Ingredients

- ½ cup of unsalted butter
- 1 ½ cups of graham cracker crumbs
- 1 cup of semisweet chocolate chips
- 1 cup of butterscotch chips
- 1 cup of chop up walnuts
- 1 (14 ounce) can sweetened condensed milk
- 1 ⅓ cups of shredded coconut

Directions

1. Set the oven to 350 degrees Fahrenheit (175 degrees C).
2. Melt the butter in a 13x9-inch baking dish in the oven. Butter should be swirled into the bottom and sides.
3. Sprinkle graham cracker crumbs equally across the pan's bottom. Over the crumbs, spread out the chocolate, butterscotch, and walnut chips. Coconut should be sprinkled on top of the condensed milk and walnuts.
4. Bake for about 25 minutes, or until edges are golden brown, in a preheated oven.
5. Slice into 36 bars after cooling.

24. CRUSTLESS CRANBERRY PIE

Prep Time:15 mins

Cook Time:40 mins

Total Time:55 mins

Ingredients

- 1 cup of all-purpose flour
- 1 cup of white sugar
- ¼ tsp salt
- 2 cups of cranberries

- ½ cup of chop up walnuts
- ½ cup of butter, melted
- 2 large eggs, beaten
- 1 tsp almond extract

Directions

1. Set the oven to 350 degrees Fahrenheit (175 degrees C). Butter a 9-inch pie pan.
2. In a bowl, mix the flour, sugar, and salt. Toss in the walnuts and cranberries to coat.
3. Add butter, eggs, and almond essence after mixing.
4. Pour the batter into the pan as it is ready.
5. For about 40 minutes, or until a toothpick inserted close to the middle comes out clean, bake in the preheated oven. Serve hot.

Tips

- Fresh cranberries can be swapped out for refrigerated ones, but the batter will become very thick.

25. BROWN SUGAR AND PINEAPPLE GLAZED HAM

Cook Time:1 hrs 30 mins

Total Time:1 hrs 50 mins

Ingredients

- 1 (6 pound) fully-cooked, bone-in ham
- 1 fresh pineapple
- 2 (6 ounce) cans pineapple juice
- 1 cup of brown sugar

Directions

1. Set the oven to 325 degrees Fahrenheit (165 degrees C). Put the ham in the roasting pan slice-side down.
2. Slice off any brown areas or skin that remains after using a sharp knife to remove the pineapple's skin. Using a round cutter, slice pineapple into 1/2-inch-thick rings and remove the cores. Use toothpicks to attach rings to the ham.

3. For 30 minutes, bake the ham in the preheated oven.

4. Mix pineapple juice and brown sugar in a basin that is microwave-safe while the ham bakes. Melt glaze in the microwave on medium power until it boils and starts to thicken. Work cautiously as the glaze will be hot and sticky.

5. Over the ham and pineapple rings, evenly pour half of the glaze. After another 30 minutes of baking, brush the ham with the leftover glaze.

6. Ham should continue baking for a further 30 to 60 minutes, or until a meat thermometer inserted into the thickest portion of the ham registers 140 degrees F (60 degrees C).

26. EASY CRANBERRY ORANGE RELISH

Prep Time:10 mins

Additional Time:2 hrs

Total Time:2 hrs 10 mins

Ingredients

- 1 medium navel orange
- 1 (12 ounce) package fresh cranberries
- ½ cup of white sugar
- ⅛ tsp ground cinnamon

Directions

1. Orange peel and pith should be discarded after grating 2 tsp of orange zest. Orange should be slice up.

2. In a food processor, mix orange sections, 2 tsp orange zest, cranberries, sugar, and cinnamon; process until the ingredients are lightly chop up.

Put relish in a bowl. Cover and chill for at least two hours and as long as three days to allow flavors to meld.

27. HAM WITH PINEAPPLE

Prep Time:20 mins

Cook Time: 4 hrs

Total Time: 4 hrs 20 mins

Ingredients

- 1 (12 pound) bone-in ham
- ½ cup of whole cloves
- 1 (20 ounce) can pineapple rings in heavy syrup
- 1 (12 fluid ounce) can or bottle lemon-lime flavored carbonated beverage
- ½ cup of packed brown sugar
- 1 (4 ounce) jar chop up maraschino cherries

Directions

1. Set the oven to 325 degrees Fahrenheit (160 degrees C).
2. In a roasting pan, put the ham. Score the ham rind in a diamond pattern with a sharp knife. Every diamond's center should include a clove.
3. To the pineapple juice in a medium bowl, add lemon-lime soda and brown sugar and whisk to mix. Apply the juice mixture on the ham, then place the pineapple rings on it. Every pineapple ring should include a maraschino cherry in the center, which you should toothpick in place.
4. Bake uncovered, basting regularly with pan juices, in the preheated oven for 4 to 5 hours, or until the internal temperature of the ham reaches 160°F (72°C). Make sure the bone is not in contact with the meat thermometer.
5. Before serving, remove the toothpicks.

28. SPINACH AND BANANA POWER SMOOTHIE

Prep Time: 10 mins

Total Time: 10 mins

Servings: 1

Ingredients

- 1 cup of plain soy milk
- ¾ cup of packed fresh spinach leaves
- 1 large banana, split

Directions

1. Spinach and soy milk should be blended until smooth. Banana is added; pulse until well-mixd.
2. Cook's Notes: If you like, you can use vanilla soy milk instead of plain soy milk.
3. Most of us are aware of spinach's health benefits. But let's face it, nobody wants to have a spinach salad every day. Because you won't even taste the greens in this smoothie, bananas are truly a wonder meal. It's a fantastic way to consume fresh spinach and get all of its nutritional advantages without ever realizing it.

29. GINGERBREAD COOKIE FROSTING

Prep Time:10 mins

Total Time:10 mins

Servings:4

Ingredients

- 1 cup of confectioners' sugar
- ¼ cup of milk, or as needed
- 10 drops food coloring

Directions

1. Put confectioners' sugar in a little bowl by sifting it.
2. Add just enough milk to achieve the right consistency—smooth but not runny.
3. Depending on how many colors you desire, divide the mixture into tiny containers. Fill every container with food coloring, using as much as necessary to achieve the desired shades.

Tips

- If, after adding milk, the frosting's consistency becomes too runny, you might need to correct it by adding additional sugar.

30. CARAMEL APPLES

Prep Time:8 mins

Cook Time:2 mins

Additional Time:15 mins

Total Time:25 mins

Servings:6

Ingredients

- 6 apples
- 6 wooden craft sticks
- cooking spray
- 1 (14 ounce) package individually wrapped caramels, unwrapped
- 2 tbsp milk

Directions

1. Every apple's stem should be removed before inserting a craft stick into the top. Apply cooking spray on a baking sheet.

2. In a bowl that can go in the microwave, mix the milk and caramels. Microwave for 2 minutes, stirring once. Put aside for a while to cool.

3. Every apple should be rapidly coated with caramel sauce. To set, place on prepared sheet.

31. PINEAPPLE STUFFING

Prep Time:5 mins

Cook Time:1 hrs

Total Time:1 hrs 5 mins

Ingredients

- 1 cup of white sugar
- ½ cup of butter or margarine
- 4 eggs
- 1 (20 ounce) can crushed pineapple, drained
- 5 slices white bread, cubed

Directions

1. Set the oven to 350 degrees Fahrenheit (175 degrees C). Butter a 9-inch baking dish.
2. In a large basin, blend sugar and butter; use an electric mixer to beat until smooth and creamy. One at a time, beat in the eggs. Next, toss in the pineapple and the bread cubes. Finally, pour the mixture into the prepared baking dish.
3. Bake for one hour in the preheated oven. Before serving, let it rest for a few minutes to firm up.

32. AWESOME SAUSAGE, APPLE AND CRANBERRY STUFFING

Prep Time: 15 mins

Cook Time: 15 mins

Additional Time: 1 hrs

Total Time: 1 hrs 30 mins

Ingredients

- 3 ¾ cups of cubed white bread
- 1 ½ cups of cubed whole wheat bread
- 1 pound ground turkey sausage
- 1 cup of chop up onion
- ¾ cup of chop up celery
- 2 ½ tsp dried sage
- 1 ½ tsp dried rosemary

- ½ tsp dried thyme
- 1 Golden Delicious apple, cored and chop up
- ¾ cup of dried cranberries
- ⅓ cup of chop up fresh parsley
- 1 cooked turkey liver, lightly chop up
- ¾ cup of turkey stock
- 4 tbsp unsalted butter, melted

Directions

1. Set the oven to 350 degrees Fahrenheit (175 degrees C).
2. On a sizable baking sheet, arrange bread cubes made of white and whole wheat in a single layer.
3. Bake for 5 to 7 minutes, stirring once, until toasty all over. Place the cubes of toasted bread in a big basin.
4. Using a large skillet over medium heat, cook the sausage and onions for 6 to 8 minutes, breaking up any lumps as you go. Add the celery, sage, rosemary, and thyme. Cook and stir for two minutes to let the flavors meld.
5. Add the sausage mixture to the bowl of bread. Add the diced apple, parsley, liver, and dried cranberries. Add melted butter and turkey stock, and stir just enough to mix.
6. Before loosely filling a bird, let the stuffing cool to room temperature.

33. AMAZING APPLE BUTTER

Prep Time:10 mins

Cook Time:10 hrs 25 mins

Additional Time:5 mins

Total Time:10 hrs 40 mins

Ingredients

- 10 pounds apples, quartered
- 4 cups of unsweetened apple juice
- 1 cup of white sugar
- 1 tbsp apple cider vinegar

- 1 ½ tsp ground cinnamon
- ½ tsp ground cloves
- ½ tsp ground allspice
- 6 half-pint canning jars with lids and rings

Directions

1. Apples and apple juice should be mixd in a stockpot and heated to a boil. After turning down the heat, simmer the apples for 20 to 30 minutes, or until they are mushy.

2. Apples should be placed in a food processor and blended; the residual cores and peels should be thrown away. Move the cooked apples to the slow cooker.

3. Cook on High without the lid off for overnight to 24 hours, or until the volume is reduced by nearly half and the moisture has evaporated.

4. Mix the apple puree with the sugar, apple cider vinegar, cinnamon, cloves, and allspice.

5. Continue cooking on High for a further 2 to 6 hours, or until the mixture forms mounds on a cooled platter without any water separating from the borders.

6. Boiling water must be used to sterilize the jars and lids for at least five minutes. Fill the sterilized, heated jars to within 1/4 inch of the top with the apple butter. After the jars have been filled, use a knife or a tiny spatula to smooth out any air bubbles. To get rid of any food leftovers, wipe the jar rims with a wet paper towel. Place lids on top, then tighten rings.

7. A large stockpot should have a rack in the bottom and half an inch of water in the pot. Use a holder to lower the jars into the boiling water after bringing to a boil. Space the jars apart by 2 inches. If additional boiling water is required to reach a height of at least 1 inch above the jar tops, add it now. Water should be brought to a roaring boil before being covered and cooked for 5 to 10 minutes.

8. When cold, remove the jars from the stockpot and set them several inches apart on a surface covered in linen or made of wood. After cool, test the tightness of every lid's seal by pressing the top with your finger (lid does not move up or down at all). Store in a cool, enclosed space.

Cook's Note:

- Take this recipe and modify the cooking time and temperature to fit your slow cooker. In order to avoid scorching, you might need to simmer for longer or shorter periods of time, depending on the consistency you want.

34. CRANBERRY ORANGE BREAD

Prep Time: 15 mins

Cook Time: 1 hrs

Additional Time:10 mins

Total Time:1 hrs 25 mins

Ingredients

- 2 cups of flour
- ¾ cup of white sugar
- 1 ½ tsp baking powder
- ¾ tsp salt
- ½ tsp baking soda
- ¼ cup of unsalted butter, slice into pieces and softened
- ¾ cup of orange juice
- 1 tbsp grated orange zest
- 1 large egg, beaten
- 1 cup of chop up cranberries
- ½ cup of chop up walnuts (Non-compulsory)

Directions

1. Set the oven to 350 degrees Fahrenheit (175 degrees C). An 8 1/2x4 1/2-inch loaf pan should be greased.
2. In a bowl, mix together the flour, sugar, baking powder, salt, and baking soda. Mixture of flour and butter should be mixed. Orange juice, orange zest, and egg should all be added.
3. Mix walnuts and cranberries. Batter is poured into the prepared pan.
4. Bake in the preheated oven for 60 to 75 minutes, or until a toothpick inserted in the center comes out clean.
5. Before transferring to totally cool on a wire rack, let the food sit in the pan for 10 minutes.
6. Making Muffins
7. Pour the batter into muffin tins that have been buttered, and bake for 15 to 20 minutes at 375 degrees F (190 degrees C).

35. GREEK LEMON CHICKEN SOUP

Prep Time:20 mins

Cook Time:30 mins

Total Time:50 mins

Servings:16

Ingredients

- 8 cups of chicken broth
- ½ cup of fresh lemon juice
- ½ cup of shredded carrots
- ½ cup of lightly chop up onion
- ½ cup of lightly chop up celery
- 6 tbsp chicken soup base
- ¼ tsp ground white pepper
- ¼ cup of margarine
- ¼ cup of all-purpose flour
- 8 egg yolks
- 1 cup of cooked white rice
- 1 cup of diced, cooked chicken meat
- 16 slices lemon

Directions

1. In a big saucepan, mix chicken broth, lemon juice, celery, carrots, onions, soup base, and white pepper. When the vegetables are ready, simmer for 15 to 20 minutes after bringing to a boil over high heat.

2. In a separate bowl, mix the flour and margarine; add gradually into the soup mixture. Simmer for 8 to 10 minutes while stirring often.

3. Egg yolks should be beaten in a bowl until they are light in color. Using a ladle to pour in a thin stream of hot soup while quickly whisking the egg yolks. In the same way, add the egg mixture to the pot and heat it through.

4. Stir in the rice and chicken, then heat everything through. Pour heated soup into bowls, top with lemon slices, and serve.

Tips

- You might not need to add more chicken base if the chicken broth you're using is already flavorful. After completing step 1, we advise tasting the soup and adding chicken base as desired.

36. HOMEMADE BANANA PUDDING

Prep Time: 10 mins

Cook Time: 20 mins

Additional Time: 1 hrs

Total Time: 1 hrs 30 mins

Ingredients

- ⅔ cup of white sugar
- ⅓ cup of all-purpose flour
- ¼ tsp salt
- 3 eggs, beaten
- 2 cups of milk
- 2 tbsp butter, softened
- ½ tsp vanilla extract
- 2 bananas, peel off and split
- ½ (12 ounce) package vanilla wafer cookies

Directions

1. In a medium saucepan, mix together the flour, sugar, and salt. Stir well after adding eggs. Add milk and simmer while continually stirring over low heat.

2. When the mixture has thickened enough to coat the back of a metal spoon, remove from heat and continue to stir, cooling slightly. Add vanilla and butter, and stir until smooth.

3. In a serving dish, mix pudding, bananas, and vanilla wafers. Before serving, let the food chill for at least an hour in the fridge.

37. FRESH CRANBERRY SAUCE

Cook Time: 20 mins

Total Time: 20 mins

Servings: 16

Ingredients

- 1 cup of water
- 1 cup of white sugar
- 1 (12 ounce) package fresh cranberries (such as Ocean Spray®)

Directions

1. In a saucepan, bring the water to a boil. Add the sugar, and cook for 5 minutes, or until the sugar is dissolved.

2. Cranberries are added to the saucepan and heated to a boil. Lower heat to low and simmer for 10 minutes or more, depending on desired consistency, or until cranberries have popped and sauce is chunky. It will be less chunky the longer you simmer it.

3. The pectin in the cranberries will cause the cranberry sauce to gel as it cools. Spoon the sauce into a serving dish or jars and cover until ready to use.

4. Before serving, mash the cranberry sauce with a fork.

Tips

- You can increase the amount of white sugar in this recipe to 2 cups of if you prefer a sweeter cranberry sauce. I just use 1 cup of because I like a tangy sauce.

38. BANANA PUMPKIN BREAD

Prep Time:20 mins

Cook Time:45 mins

Total Time:1 hrs 5 mins

Servings:12

Ingredients

- 2 ripe bananas, mashed
- 1 ⅓ cups of canned pumpkin puree
- ½ cup of honey

- ½ cup of white sugar
- ⅓ cup of vegetable oil
- 2 large eggs
- 2 ½ cups of all-purpose flour
- 2 tsp pumpkin pie spice
- 1 tsp baking powder
- 1 tsp baking soda
- 1 tsp ground cinnamon
- ½ tsp salt
- ¾ cup of raisins (Non-compulsory)
- ½ cup of walnut pieces (Non-compulsory)

Directions

1. Set the oven to 350 degrees Fahrenheit (175 degrees C). Butter a 9x5-inch loaf pan.

2. Bananas, pumpkin, honey, sugar, vegetable oil, and eggs are mixd in a big bowl. In a another bowl, mix the flour, pie spice, baking powder, baking soda, cinnamon, and salt. Just mix the wheat mixture and banana combination. Mix in the walnuts and raisins. Fill the pan with the batter.

3. Around 45 minutes into baking in the preheated oven, a toothpick inserted into the center of the loaf should come out clean. Before transferring the loaf to a wire rack to finish cooling, let it sit in the pan for 10 minutes.

39. SPINACH AND STRAWBERRY SALAD

Prep Time:10 mins

Total Time:10 mins

Servings:8

Ingredients

- 2 bunches spinach, rinsed and torn into bite-size pieces
- 4 cups of split strawberries

- ½ cup of vegetable oil
- ½ cup of white sugar
- ¼ cup of white wine vinegar
- 2 tbsp sesame seeds
- 1 tbsp poppy seeds
- ¼ tsp paprika

Directions

1. Spinach and strawberries should be mixed together in a big basin.
2. In a medium bowl, mix the oil, sugar, vinegar, sesame, poppy, and paprika. Pour over the strawberries and spinach, then mix to coat.

40. DELICIOUS CINNAMON BAKED APPLES

Prep Time: 15 mins

Cook Time: 45 mins

Total Time: 1 hrs

Ingredients

- 1 tsp butter
- 2 tbsp brown sugar

- 3 tsp vanilla sugar
- 3 tsp ground cinnamon
- 1 tsp ground nutmeg
- 6 large apples - peel off, cored, and split
- 3 ½ tbsp water

Directions

1. Set the oven to 350 degrees Fahrenheit (175 degrees C). Butter should be used to grease a big baking pan.
2. In a small bowl, mix the brown sugar, vanilla sugar, cinnamon, and nutmeg.
3. On the baking dish that has been prepared, layer about 1/3 of the apples, then sprinkle with 1/3 of the sugar mixture.
4. Layers are repeated twice more.
5. Bake for 30 minutes in a preheated oven. Add water to the apples and bake for a further 15 minutes, or until apples are soft.

41. CHICKEN WITH LEMON-CAPER SAUCE

Prep Time: 10 mins

Cook Time: 20 mins

Total Time: 30 mins

Servings: 2

Ingredients

- ½ cup of all-purpose flour

- 1 pinch salt
- 2 (6 ounce) skinless, boneless chicken breast halves
- 2 tbsp olive oil
- ¼ cup of dry white wine
- ¼ cup of lemon juice
- ¼ cup of cold unsalted butter, slice into pieces
- 2 tbsp capers, drained
- 2 lemon wedges

Directions

1. In a medium bowl or sealable plastic bag, mix flour and salt. Shake off extra flour after coating the chicken.

2. In a skillet, heat the olive oil over medium-high heat. Sauté chicken in heated oil for 3 to 4 minutes on every side, or until golden brown and well done. In the center, an instant-read thermometer should register at least 165 degrees Fahrenheit (74 degrees C). Place the chicken on a platter, cover it, and maintain warmth.

3. White wine should be added to the skillet and brought to a boil while the cooked bits are being scraped from the bottom of the pan. Add lemon juice and cook for 2 to 3 minutes, or until reduced by half.

4. In the sauce that is boiling, add diced butter. Shake and swirl the pan erratically until the sauce thickens and the butter is fully absorbed. (Butter should never rest; else, sauce will separate and turn greasy.) Capers are added when the heat is turned off.

5. Add a lemon-caper sauce and serve the chicken with lemon wedges.

42. BLUEBERRY SIMPLE SYRUP

Prep Time:15 mins

Cook Time:20 mins

Total Time:35 mins

Ingredients

- 1 cup of blueberries

- 1 cup of warm water
- 1 cup of white sugar
- 1 tsp lemon juice

Directions

1. In a small saucepan over low heat, mix blueberries, water, and sugar until sugar is dissolved, about 5 minutes. Increasing the heat to medium-high, bring the mixture to a moderate boil for about 15 minutes while stirring often.
2. Lemon juice should be incorporated into the syrup before serving.

Tips

- Other fruit including strawberries, raspberries, and blackberries also work well with this dish. For a smoother syrup when using raspberries and blackberries, the seeds can be filtered out.
- Just before bringing the syrup to a boil, toss in a mixture of 1 tbsp cornstarch and 1/2 tbsp water to form a thicker syrup that you may use to top pancakes.

43. HOT SPIKED CIDER

Prep Time:5 mins

Cook Time:10 mins

Total Time:15 mins

Servings:6

Ingredients

- 1 quart water
- 3 orange spice tea bags
- 2 cups of apple cider
- 1 ½ cups of light rum
- ½ cup of light brown sugar
- 2 cinnamon sticks
- 3 tsp butter
- 6 cinnamon sticks, garnish

Directions

1. Large pot with water in it should be brought to a boil.
2. Add orange spice tea bags after removing from the heat. For five minutes, cover and let steep.
3. Take out the tea bags and then whisk in the rum, brown sugar, apple cider, and two cinnamon sticks. Cider should only be steaming after being heated on low heat.
4. Pour 6 mugs with hot cider and add 1/2 tsp of butter to every. Add a cinnamon "swizzle" stick as garnish.

44. ALMOST NO FAT BANANA BREAD

Prep Time:10 mins

Cook Time:55 mins

Total Time:1 hrs 5 mins

Servings:12

Ingredients

- cooking spray
- 1 ½ cups of all-purpose flour
- ¾ cup of white sugar
- 1 ¼ tsp baking powder
- ½ tsp baking soda
- ½ tsp ground cinnamon
- 1 cup of banana, mashed
- ¼ cup of applesauce
- 2 egg whites

Directions

1. Set the oven to 350 degrees Fahrenheit (175 degrees C). Grease an 8x4-inch loaf pan very lightly.
2. In a big basin, mix the flour, sugar, baking soda, baking powder, and cinnamon. Egg whites, applesauce, and banana should all be added. Stir just until incorporated. Fill the pan with the batter.

3. Bake in a preheated oven for 50 to 55 minutes, or until a toothpick inserted in the center comes out clean. Before slicing, turn out onto a wire rack and let cool.

45. THREE BERRY PIE

Prep Time:45 mins

Cook Time:45 mins

Additional Time:1 day 21 hrs

Total Time:1 day 22 hrs 30 mins

Ingredients

Double Pie Crust:

- 2 cups of all-purpose flour
- ½ tsp salt
- ⅔ cup of shortening, chilled
- 6 tbsp cold water

Berry Filling:

- ½ cup of white sugar
- 3 tbsp cornstarch
- 2 cups of fresh raspberries
- 1 ½ cups of fresh blueberries
- 1 cup of fresh strawberries, halved

Directions

1. creating the crust Salt and flour should be mixd in a big bowl. Using two knives or a pastry cutter, blend in cold shortening until the mixture resembles coarse crumbs. Tossing with a fork, add water, 1 tbsp at a time, until the flour mixture is wet. Do not add more water than is necessary; a ball should form when you press a handful of the moistened pastry mixture. Create balls by dividing the dough in half. Put in the fridge for at least 30 minutes after wrapping in plastic wrap.

2. One dough ball should be transferred to a gently dusted surface. To create a 12-inch circle, roll the dough from the center outward. Rolling pin should be wrapped in crust. Onto a 9-inch pie pan, unroll it. Avoid stretching the crust as you gently press it into the pie pan. Return the pie plate with the pastry lining to the refrigerator after trimming the bottom crust to match the rim.

3. Creating the filling Cornstarch and sugar are mixd in a sizable bowl. Strawberries, blueberries, and raspberries should be added. Gently toss to mix. Let the fruit combination roughly 15 minutes to stand.

4. In the meantime, heat the oven to 375°F (190 degrees C). Bake a sheet of bread in the preheated oven.

5. For the top crust, roll out the leftover dough. Pour the berry mixture into the pie plate after stirring. Overlay the filling with the top crust, trimming the sides to leave a 1/2-inch overhang. With a light press, tuck the top crust under the bottom crust. To let steam out, crimp the edges and slice vents at the top. Cover the edges with foil to stop them from getting too brown.

6. For 25 minutes, bake the food on the baking sheet in the preheated oven. After about 20 minutes, take the foil off and continue baking until the crust is brown and the filling is bubbling.

Tips

- Instead of raspberries, you may use fresh blackberries.

- Using refrigerated fruit is an alternative to fresh berries; simply lengthen the baking time. Pie should be baked for 50 minutes, then with the foil removed, for a further 40 minutes, or until the pastry is golden and the contents is bubbling.

46. LEMON-ORANGE ORANGE ROUGHY

Prep Time: 10 mins

Cook Time: 5 mins

Total Time: 15 mins

Ingredients

- 1 tbsp olive oil
- 4 (4 ounce) fillets orange roughy
- 1 orange, juiced
- 1 lemon, juiced
- ½ tsp lemon pepper

Directions

1. In a sizable skillet, heat the oil over medium-high heat.

2. Fillets are placed in heated oil. Orange and lemon juice should be drizzled over the fillets before lemon pepper. Sauté for 2 to 3 minutes on every side or until salmon flakes easily with a fork. In the center, an instant-read thermometer should register at least 145 degrees Fahrenheit (63 degrees C).

47. IRISH POTATO CANDY

Prep Time:20 mins

Additional Time:10 mins

Total Time:30 mins

Servings:60

Ingredients

- 4 ounces cream cheese, softened
- ¼ cup of butter, softened
- 4 cups of confectioners' sugar
- 1 tsp vanilla extract
- 2 ½ cups of flaked coconut
- 1 tbsp ground cinnamon

Directions

1. Cream cheese and butter are mixd and smoothed out in a big basin. Beat until smooth after adding vanilla and confectioners' sugar. Mix with coconut flake.
2. Form mixture into potatoes or balls, and then roll the balls in cinnamon. Put the ingredients on a cookie sheet and chill for at least 10 minutes to set. Potatoes can be coated with cinnamon once more for a deeper shade if preferred.

48. DUTCH APPLE PIE WITH OATMEAL STREUSEL

Prep Time:15 mins

Cook Time:45 mins

Total Time:1 hrs

Servings:8

Yield:

Ingredients

Apple Pie:

- 5 cups of apples - peel off, cored and split
- ⅔ cup of white sugar
- 2 tbsp all-purpose flour
- ½ tsp ground cinnamon
- ¼ tsp ground nutmeg
- ¼ tsp ground allspice
- 1 (9 inch) refrigerated pie crust
- 2 tbsp butter
- aluminum foil

Streusel Topping:

- ¾ cup of all-purpose flour
- ¾ cup of rolled oats
- ½ cup of packed brown sugar
- 1 tsp lemon zest
- ½ tsp ground cinnamon
- ½ cup of butter

Directions

1. Set the oven to 425 degrees Fahrenheit (220 degrees C).
2. Creating the apple pie A big bowl should contain apple slices. In a separate bowl, mix the white sugar, flour, cinnamon, nutmeg, and allspice; sprinkle over the apples, and toss to coat.
3. Take the pie shell out of the freezer, fill it with the apple mixture, and top it with butter. Place a thin layer of aluminum foil on top of the filling; do not seal.
4. For ten minutes, bake the pie in a preheated oven.
5. Make the streusel topping in the interim: In a larger bowl, mix the flour, oats, brown sugar, lemon zest, and cinnamon. Once the mixture is crumbly, slice in the butter. Pie should be taken out of the oven with streusel on top.
6. Heat to 375 degrees Fahrenheit (190 degrees C). Bake the pie for an additional 30 to 35 minutes, or until the apples are soft and the streusel is golden. Aluminum foil should be used loosely to prevent overbrowning.

49. MINCEMEAT

Prep Time:10 mins

Cook Time:10 mins

Additional Time:30 mins

Total Time:50 mins

Ingredients

Mixed Spice:

- 1 tsp ground cinnamon
- 1 tsp ground cloves
- 1 tsp ground ginger
- 1 tsp ground nutmeg
- 1 tsp ground allspice

Mincemeat:

- 1 large green apple, peel off and lightly chop up
- 1 ¼ cups of sultana raisins
- 1 ⅛ cups of white sugar
- ½ cup of dried currants
- ½ cup of raisins
- ½ cup of butter
- ½ cup of chop up almonds
- 1 ½ tbsp grated orange zest
- ½ tsp ground cinnamon
- 1 cup of brandy

Directions

1. Mix the spices in a bowl by combining the cinnamon, cloves, ginger, nutmeg, and allspice. For the mincemeat, set aside 1 heaping tsp. For later use, put the remainder in a little jar.

2. Until mincemeat is done, cook two clean 12-ounce jars in water. With warm, soapy water, clean new, unused lids and rings.

3. Apple, sultanas, sugar, currants, raisins, and butter are mixd in a skillet to make mincemeat. Simmer and stir slowly over low heat until butter has melted. Add cinnamon, orange zest, 1 tsp mixed spices, and split almonds. Stirring occasionally, bring mixture to a simmer and simmer for 5 to 10 minutes.

4. Mincemeat should be taken off the heat and left to cool for 30 minutes. Add brandy and stir. Spoon contents into sterile jars.

Tips

- Use only jars that are devoid of any rust or cracks.
- Brandy can be substituted with orange juice.

50. BEST BOILED FRUITCAKE

Prep Time: 15 mins

Cook Time: 2 hrs 20 mins

Additional Time: 5 mins

Total Time: 2 hrs 40 mins

Ingredients

- 1 ½ cups of white sugar
- 12 ounces candied mixed fruit
- 1 cup of milk
- ¾ cup of butter
- 5 ounces glace cherries, roughly chop up
- 2 ounces candied mixed citrus peel
- 2 ounces chop up walnuts
- 1 tsp ground allspice
- ½ tsp baking soda
- 12 ounces sifted self-rising flour
- 2 large eggs

Directions

1. Set the oven to 325 degrees Fahrenheit (160 degrees C). Use parchment paper to line an 8-inch deep cake pan.

2. In a medium-sized saucepan, mix the sugar, milk, butter, cherries, citrus peel, walnuts, allspice, and candied mixed fruit. Boil for a few minutes, then turn down the heat and simmer for five. Take from heat and give it a little time to cool.

3. Fruit combination is blended with wheat and eggs. Fill the pan with the batter. Using newspaper or brown paper, cover the pan's exterior.

4. Cake should be baked for 40 minutes in a preheated oven. To continue baking the cake, lower the temperature to 300 degrees F (150 degrees C) and bake it for 1 1/2 hours.

5. After allowing the cake to set at room temperature for five minutes, flip it over onto a wire rack. Flip the cake over, take off the parchment paper, and let it finish cooling on the rack. For up to six months, cake can be kept wrapped in foil and in an airtight container.

Made in United States
Troutdale, OR
04/14/2025